Online Addiction

Patricia D. Netzley

ReferencePoint Press®

San Diego, CA

About the Author
Patricia D. Netzley is the author of dozens of books for children, teens, and adults. She also teaches writing and is a member of the Society of Children's Book Writers and Illustrators.

© 2017 ReferencePoint Press, Inc.
Printed in the United States

For more information, contact:
ReferencePoint Press, Inc.
PO Box 27779
San Diego, CA 92198
www.ReferencePointPress.com

LIBRARY OF CONGRESS CATALOGING-IN-PUBLICATION DATA

Names: Netzley, Patricia D.
Title: Online addiction / by Patricia D. Netzley.
Description: San Diego, CA : ReferencePoint Press, Inc., 2017. | Series: Digital issues series | Audience: Grade 9 to 12. | Includes bibliographical references and index.
Identifiers: LCCN 2016011960 (print) | LCCN 2016014585 (ebook) | ISBN 9781601529848 (hardback) | ISBN 9781601529855 (eBook)
Subjects: LCSH: Internet addiction--Juvenile literature.
Classification: LCC RC569.5.I54 N482 2017 (print) | LCC RC569.5.I54 (ebook) DDC 616.85/84--dc23
LC record available at http://lccn.loc.gov/2016011960

CONTENTS

Introduction   4
From Pastime to Compulsion

Chapter One   8
The Nature of Online Addiction

Chapter Two   19
The Causes of Online Addiction

Chapter Three   32
The Physical Consequences of
Online Addiction

Chapter Four   44
Living with an Online Addiction

Chapter Five   54
Breaking an Online Addiction

Source Notes   67

Organizations to Contact   72

For Further Research   74

Index   76

Picture Credits   80

From Pastime to Compulsion

A t least 2 billion people across the globe own smart-phones, and in the United States the number of smart-phone users is expected to top 220 million by 2018. Today roughly two out of three Americans own smartphones—up from just one in six in 2004. This dramatic rise in portable online access has led to corresponding increases in online addiction, which is generally described as compulsive engagement in online activities that interfere with normal living.

The way Michael Saylor, author of *The Mobile Wave: How Mobile Intelligence Will Change Everything*, uses his smartphone is typical of many who struggle with online addiction. "I must look at it 500 times a day, or 1,000 times a day," he reports, adding that very few things would make him stop this behavior. "If I was with the queen of England and she was addressing me directly and it was a one-on-one conversation, then I would probably discipline myself to not look at my phone, so as to not show disrespect to her,"[1] he says. Otherwise he would keep checking for e-mails and texts.

Saylor is not alone in this behavior. According to a 2015 Gallup poll, 81 percent of smartphone owners in the United States keep their devices with them at all times. For some this is simply a matter of convenience, but for others it represents a dependence that is hard to shake.

"A Phantom Limb"

As an example of the degree to which people, especially youth, are dependent on their devices, some teens have difficulty completing the Tech Timeout Academic Challenge, which calls on students to go without digital devices for three days. Ryley Aceret, a high school student in San Francisco who took the challenge in 2015, failed it because being without his smartphone was too upsetting. During the first hours of the challenge he felt "jittery, like I'm on drugs or something,"[2] and as time went on he became increasingly anxious. "When I wasn't with my phone I felt different, like I was naked all the time,"[3] he says.

> "I must look at [my phone] 500 times a day, or 1,000 times a day."[1]
>
> —Michael Saylor, author of *The Mobile Wave: How Mobile Intelligence Will Change Everything.*

Experts say this type of discomfort is common. "Technology has become like a phantom limb," says Sherry Turkle, an expert on how technology impacts individuals and society. "These young people are among the first to grow up with an expectation of continuous connection: always on, and always on them."[4] Sixteen-year-old Philippa Grogan of the United Kingdom is an example of someone who feels this way. She says, "I'd rather give up, like, a kidney than my phone."[5]

The Inflection Point

Experts who study dependence on technology say that when a person's engagement in online activities goes from being a want to a need, he or she can be considered addicted to those activities. The moment when this happens is known as the inflection point. At this moment, something that was once harmless can become harmful.

Reaching the inflection point can be a gradual process. For example, a man might buy a phone purely for safety reasons, in order to reach someone in an emergency. After awhile he starts using the phone to make other kinds of calls. Then one day he decides to send a text instead of making a call, and soon he is texting regularly. Eventually this habit becomes so ingrained that

Many people like working on tablets because they are easy to use, portable, and convenient. These same qualities can lead users astray—to the point of being obsessed with e-mail and games.

he cannot stop texting even while driving. His need to do this—at the expense of his safety, the very thing he bought the phone to maintain—shows that his habit has tipped over into addiction.

Shame and Secrecy

Years ago, most addiction experts did not believe that people could become addicted to accessing the Internet. Today, however, that idea is widely accepted, with some experts noting that such online addictions share some of the behavioral hallmarks of drug addictions. For example, both drug and Internet addiction can involve a gradual escalation of use accompanied by a great deal of secrecy and shame.

This was the case with a therapist who became addicted to using a tablet computer to play Internet games. He bought an iPad for work purposes but soon found himself obsessed with answering not just work e-mails but personal ones as well. Then he downloaded some gaming apps, became hooked on playing the games

Angry Birds and *Fruit Ninja,* and began to hide his online behavior from his wife. In an anonymous blog post he writes, "I was struck at how easy it was to become engrossed with my new toy (I mean — business tool!) and I knew things were going sideways when I, shamefully, found myself hurriedly trying to fumble through shutting down or hiding my iPad when I could hear her coming home."[6]

Negative Consequences

Such behavior often strains the relationships of online addicts, and not just because one partner is keeping secrets from the other. Online activities can lead someone to neglect a relationship until it is damaged beyond repair. Other negative consequences of online addictions include financial hardship from money lost in online gaming and gambling, physical injury from dangerous activities like texting while driving, and problems holding a job or doing well in school.

Experts say these fates can be avoided by ending or at least cutting back on addictive online behaviors before the inflection point is reached. This is because the inflection point is like a point of no return — once it has been passed, it is much harder to go back to being online in moderation. Contributing to this difficulty is the fact that whereas people with alcohol or drug addictions can avoid going places where alcohol and drugs are present, the nature of contemporary life is such that Internet addicts often cannot avoid encountering or using computer technology.

> "I'd rather give up, like, a kidney than my phone."[5]
>
> —Sixteen-year-old smartphone user Philippa Grogan of the United Kingdom.

Another problem that Internet addicts and potential addicts face is that there are no guidelines as to how much online use is too much. Marc Potenza, an addiction specialist at Yale University explains, "The truth is, we don't know what's normal. It's not like alcohol where we have healthy amounts that we can recommend to people."[7] However, experts do say that whenever a person feels as though the Internet is having a negative effect on his or her life, it is time to seek help.

CHAPTER ONE

The Nature of Online Addiction

Ever since the Internet became accessible to the public in the 1990s, users have reported feeling addicted to going online. In fact, people who owned a BlackBerry, one of the earliest smartphones, often joked that it should be called the CrackBerry because of its addictive properties. Nonetheless, for years addiction experts resisted using the word *addiction* to refer to uncontrollable behaviors related to online activities. Instead, these experts insisted—and some still insist—that excessive Internet use be called a dependency, obsession, or compulsion.

The main reason is because *addiction* has long been used to describe the excessive and harmful abuse of drugs and/or alcohol. The American Psychiatric Association (APA) has classified drug and alcohol addictions as mental illnesses. Therefore, some experts worry that if spending a lot of time on the Internet is deemed an addiction, people whose online habits are excessive but not harmful might be considered mentally ill as well. As prominent psychiatrist Allen Frances notes, "It's a slippery slope. When you turn people's passions and interests into mental disorders, you start to define what's normal and what's not."[8]

Despite such concerns, beginning in the 2000s prominent individuals in the medical community called for the APA to recognize Internet dependency as an addiction. Some have asked the APA to include a diagnosis of Internet addiction in its *Diagnostic and Statistical Manual* of *Mental Disorders*, though the APA has repeatedly refused to do so. Nonetheless, passionate discussions surrounding the idea have caused many medical professionals to reconsider their resistance to it.

As a result, today many experts feel comfortable referring to Internet dependency as an Internet addiction, and there is now a common definition of what constitutes this addiction. According to the Center for Internet Addiction, a treatment center for Internet addicts, such addictions are "any online-related, compulsive behavior which interferes with normal living and causes severe stress on family, friends, loved ones, and one's work environment."[9]

> "When you turn people's passions and interests into mental disorders, you start to define what's normal and what's not."[8]
>
> —Psychiatrist Allen Frances.

Dominating Daily Life

Michael Murphy (not his real name) experienced this phenomenon firsthand as a sophomore at the University of Miami in 2014. He became hooked on playing an online video game called *League of Legends* (*LoL*). A free download, this fast-paced game groups players into teams of five before each match, giving it a social component that can cause many players to make friends.

Murphy says that one of his *LoL* friends warned him the game could be addictive, but he laughed off the suggestion. Then he began to experience worrisome changes in behavior. He reports,

> I would spend hours behind my screen, so many that I bought eyedrops to keep my eyes from itching to the point where I couldn't play. Half the floor was covered with dirty laundry. I'd grab a shirt off the floor . . . if I did end up leaving my apartment. My pantry held mostly microwavable food that I could make in the time I had to wait while I connected to the [Internet] server and was matched with opponents. My room was full of reeking bowls of leftover Ramen Noodles, now crusted and inedible, and red Solo cups full of old SpaghettiOs.[10]

A gamer gives his full attention to the screen. Some video games are addictive; when a player starts ignoring routine activities, like washing laundry and eating meals, these could be signs of addiction.

Murphy could not stop thinking about the game, even when others were trying to talk to him. As a result he became detached from those around him and spent less and less time with friends, telling them he had to study when he was actually going to play *LoL*.

Such actions are common for people who suffer from an Internet addiction. However, as the Center for Internet Addiction notes, "No single behavior pattern defines Internet addiction."[11] In other words, whereas some addicts might display the symptoms that Murphy did, others might display different ones, or the same ones to different degrees.

Moreover, some might spend far less time engaged in online activities than others yet feel just as addicted. This was the case for Tony Schwartz, an expert on workplace issues. Although he checked his e-mails frequently during the day and often went online to search for the latest news—particularly about politics—he did not exhibit the kind of excessive behavior that the average person would think would signal an addiction. Nonetheless, he decided he was addicted because of the way his Internet use affected his daily life. In describing the moment he realized he was an addict, he says,

> One evening . . . I opened a book and found myself reading the same paragraph over and over, a half dozen times before concluding that it was hopeless to continue. I simply couldn't marshal the necessary focus. I was horrified. All my life, reading books has been a deep and consistent source of pleasure, learning and solace. Now the books I regularly purchased were piling up ever higher on my bedside table, staring at me in silent rebuke. Instead of reading them, I was spending too many hours online.[12]

Given such cases, the Center for Internet Addiction says, "It is not the actual time spent online that determines if you have a problem [with Internet addiction], but rather how that time you spend impacts your life."[13]

However, this makes the problem of Internet addiction more widespread. "Addiction is the relentless pull to a substance or an activity that becomes so compulsive it ultimately interferes with everyday life," says Schwartz. "By that definition, nearly everyone I know is addicted in some measure to the Internet. It has arguably replaced work itself as our most socially sanctioned addiction."[14]

> "It is not the actual time spent online that determines if you have a problem, but rather how that time you spend impacts your life."[13]
>
> —Center for Internet Addiction.

A Social Addiction

Schwartz disconnected his phone and laptop from both his e-mail account and the Internet until he could get his life more in balance. Similarly, Murphy dealt with his *LoL* addiction by deleting the game from his computer and fighting the urge to return to playing it. As a result, Schwartz and Murphy both lost personal connections and relationships that had resulted from their online use.

In studying what people become addicted to, researchers have found that e-mailing, gaming, and other activities with a social component are far more addictive than those that do not feature interactions with others. This relationship component to online activities bonds people together to the point where they tend to go online more often and stay online for longer periods of time. Interestingly, relationships are also a big factor in drawing individuals back into an activity they thought they had quit.

Many online addictions have a relationship component. In addition to e-mailing and certain types of gaming, texting, instant messaging, blogging, and using Facebook and other social media sites are all about connecting with others. This makes them more likely to entice people into spending excessive amounts of time online than Internet activities that are solitary, such as checking newsfeeds.

Studies of online behavior reflect this difference. For example, a 2014 study of smartphone use among students at Baylor University in Waco, Texas, showed that the most time-consuming activity was texting, at 94.6 minutes a day. Next was sending e-mails, at 48.5 minutes a day, and checking Facebook, at 38.6 minutes a day. In comparison, the students spent just 34.4 minutes a day browsing the Internet.

Texting is the most time-consuming activity among younger students as well. According to a 2010 study by Nielsen, a company that studies consumer behavior, teens (ages thirteen to seventeen) send or receive an average of 3,339 texts a month, or over 6 per waking hour. Young adults (ages eighteen to twenty-four) send or receive an average of 1,630 texts a month, or 3 texts per waking hour. Female teens send or receive the most texts: an average of 4,050 texts per month. Male teens send or receive an average of 2,539.

Gender and Age

Studies have also shown gender and age differences among young people in regard to what they become addicted to and how significant their addictions will be. For example, according to

Secretive Behavior

Experts say that secrecy and shame can be signs of an addiction. Consequently, many find it worrisome that the computer security company McAfee, which regularly surveys teens about their Internet habits, has found that 70 percent of teens have done things to hide their online behavior from their parents. These include clearing their Internet browser history; closing or minimizing a browser when a parent walks into the room; deleting posts, photos, and other content; having secret e-mail accounts, separate from the one their parents know about; creating fake profiles on social media; and using their smartphones for online activities because their parents are less likely to check their phones. Other experts have noted a rise in teens' use of smartphone and tablet apps that allow them to hide photos and other content from their parents. As an example, one popular app looks and acts like a calculator—until the user keys in a password that unlocks an area where photos and other files can be stored in secret.

a 2015 Pew Research Center report that examined teens' use of social media, teens older than fourteen spend most of their social media time on Facebook, whereas younger teens prefer Instagram. Similarly, among all teens, far more girls say that Instagram is the site they use most often, whereas boys name Facebook as their most preferred site.

Studies of online addictions among adults have also revealed gender biases. For example, research shows that women are more likely than men to become addicted to Internet activities related to developing and maintaining relationships. In contrast, men are more likely to become addicted to activities related to dominance, violence, and sexual fantasy. More specifically, men are more likely to become addicted to online games, pornography, and gambling, and women are more likely to become addicted

Addictive tendencies vary by gender. Studies show that males are more likely to become addicted to online games, pornography, and gambling while females are more likely to become addicted to texting, online shopping, and social media sites such as Instagram (pictured).

to texting; sexting (texting of sexually charged messages and images); and social media, shopping, and auction sites.

Some researchers believe that these tendencies might be based on cultural influences rather than a person's gender. As the Center for Internet Addiction notes, "It seems to be a natural conclusion that attributes of gender played out online parallel the stereotypes men and women have in our society."[15] And, of course, no Internet activity or addiction is exclusive to men or to women.

Research Difficulties

The two most common Internet addictions, though, have a sexual component. These are sending sexts and accessing pornographic content. Experts say that increased use of mobile Internet devices like tablet computers and smartphones has resulted in a corresponding explosion in both of these activities. They also say that the majority of people addicted to viewing pornography online insist that the Internet is the only way they experience pornography.

A main reason for this is the privacy that Internet use often affords. Someone who is online can easily hide his or her activities from others, whether by concealing the screen or abandoning an Internet activity in an instant. Moreover, people can use the Internet in complete anonymity, with no one else online ever finding out their true identity or appearance.

In turn, this degree of privacy and anonymity has made it difficult for researchers to determine just how many people are addicted to online pornography. With many other Internet activities, such as gaming and texting, most people are more honest about answering surveys regarding their behavior. But this is not the case with activities related to online pornography because of the stigmas and illegalities associated with such activities.

A similar problem exists when trying to determine how many people engage in online gambling. Gambling addicts who have lost significant amounts of money can be reluctant to report their behavior because they are embarrassed about it and/or do not want their loved ones to find out about their precarious financial situation. This is also the case for those who have spent fortunes on pay-to-play games or games that require players to buy extra features, like additional lives, and for individuals who are addicted to online shopping or bidding in online auctions.

> "If you spend your time gambling online, maybe you have a gambling addiction, not an Internet addiction. If you spend your time shopping online, maybe it's a shopping addiction."[16]
>
> —*New Yorker* magazine contributor Maria Konnikova.

Is It the Internet or Something Else?

But calling online gambling or shopping Internet addictions begs the question: is it the Internet that is addictive, or is it the gambling or shopping? In addressing such questions, Maria Konnikova, who writes on issues related to science, technology, and psychology for the *New Yorker*, notes, "The Internet, after all, is a medium, not an activity in and of itself. If you spend your time gambling online, maybe you have a gambling addiction, not an Internet addiction. If you spend your time shopping online, maybe it's a shopping addiction."[16] Psychiatrist Marc Potenza calls this line of thinking the idea "that the Internet is a vehicle and not a target of disorder."[17]

A Global Problem

Thanks to the spread of technology, excessive Internet use has become a problem everywhere in the world. In several countries, in fact, a significant percent of the population reports being connected to the Internet at all times (whether via smartphone, personal computer, or tablet computer).

According to a 2014 survey by A.T. Kearney, a global management consulting firm, the two countries with the largest percent of continuously connected people are Brazil, at 51 percent, and Nigeria, at 37 percent, as compared to 25 percent in the United States. Brazil and Nigeria also have the most frequent Internet users, with 71 percent in Brazil and 66 percent in Nigeria going online at least once an hour (in the United States, 51 percent report doing this.) In addition, the survey found that the most frequent and highly connected users spend the majority of their online time on social networking, with 58 percent of Brazilians and 57 percent of Nigerians reporting this as their most time-consuming activity, compared to 39 percent in the United States.

Konnikova suggests that the same reasoning could be applied to online addictions involving relationships and connecting with others. She wonders, "Can you be addicted to a longing for virtual connectivity in the same way that you can be addicted to a longing for a drink?"[18] If this is the case, then it is connectivity the person is addicted to, not using the Internet.

danah boyd, an expert on social and cultural issues arising from technology, firmly believes that people can become addicted to connectivity. "This is why many of our youth turn to technology," she says. "They aren't addicted to the computer; they're addicted to interaction, and being around their friends."[19] She explains that children, and especially teenagers, make sense of the world by socializing with their peers. But because parents are increasingly afraid to let their children explore outside, walk the streets, or just hang out with friends unsupervised, young people are forced to rely on technology for interconnectivity. The same can be said of adults who lead relatively isolated lives.

Addicted to Information

Experts have also suggested that the Internet is not actually addictive to people who excessively search for facts or check up on the latest news. Perhaps, they propose, these individuals hunger for information the same way that others hunger for relationships. As evidence of this, they point to cases where hypochondriacs—people who have an excessive preoccupation with their health—become hooked on searching the Internet for information about symptoms they believe they have. This behavior has become so common that experts have come up with a name for it: cyberchondria.

Many people look for health information online. But some, known as cyberchondriacs, are determined to find evidence online that they are experiencing symptoms of some sort of illness.

Studies have shown that eight out of ten Americans seek health information online. According to a Harvard University study reported in 2015, two-thirds of those who engage in this behavior are anxious about their health but do not actually have a medical problem. Often the information they find online increases their anxiety, and some go on to develop full-blown cyberchondria, a condition whereby they search for information on one ailment after another.

Thomas Fergus, an assistant professor of psychology and neuroscience at Baylor University who has researched this condition, reports that people who fear the unknown are more likely to develop cyberchondria. "If I'm someone who doesn't like uncertainty, I may become more anxious, search further, monitor my body more, go to the doctor more frequently—and the more you search, the more you consider the possibilities," he says. "If I see a site about traumatic brain injuries and have difficulties tolerating uncertainty, I might be more likely to worry that's the cause of the bump on my head."[20]

Emotions, then, can determine which online activities are most likely to entice a particular person into spending enough time online to develop an addiction. Anxiety about health can lead to excessive Internet searches. Loneliness can lead to excessive texting, e-mailing, or chatting. Boredom can lead to excessive gaming. A longing for wealth can lead to excessive gambling. Whatever a person's emotional state, the Internet provides numerous ways to satisfy a person's needs and wants—which, some experts say, only adds to its addictive nature.

> "[Young people] aren't addicted to the computer; they're addicted to interaction, and being around their friends."[19]
>
> —Danah Boyd, author of *It's Complicated: The Social Life of Networked Teens.*

CHAPTER TWO

The Causes of Online Addiction

For many years, research on online addiction was scant. In fact, much work remains to determine the causes of such addictions. In part this is because few studies were undertaken during the years when Internet addiction was not considered a real addiction. But it is also because the ways in which people access and use the Internet have changed so significantly over the past decade. As Maria Konnikova of the *New Yorker* points out, Internet use "is changing too rapidly for researchers to keep up, and, though the immediate effects are fairly visible, there's no telling what the condition [of Internet addiction] will look like over the long term."[21]

Addictive Personalities

Nonetheless, addiction experts believe they have identified at least some of the causes of online addictions. It is clear that an individual's personality can determine the kind of online activities to which he or she is drawn. Psychologists Adrian F. Ward and Piercarlo Valdesolo explain: "The content of your internet usage can suggest certain psychological characteristics. Spending a lot of late nights playing high stakes internet poker? Chances are you are a risk taker. Like to post videos of yourself doing karaoke on YouTube? Clearly an extravert."[22] It appears that being addicted to online activities is connected to specific personality traits.

Indeed, studies of individuals addicted to drugs or alcohol suggest that there is such a thing as an addictive personality—a set of traits that make a person predisposed to becoming addicted. Such studies suggest that 10 to 15 percent of Americans have addictive personalities. However, experts note that it is difficult to separate the effects of personality on addiction from the effects of addiction on personality. In other words, do certain personality traits cause addiction, or are those personality traits present because the person has become addicted?

Michael Weaver, medical director of the Center for Neurobehavioral Research on Addiction at the University of Texas Health Science Center at Houston, acknowledges that this is a complex issue because, as he points out, "personalities are very complex." Nonetheless, he and many other experts think there is such a thing as an addictive personality. "While there's not one specific type that's more prone to addiction than others," he says, "there are several factors that can combine to make you more likely to become addicted."[23]

Among the most significant personality traits that have been associated with drug and alcohol addictions are impulsivity (acting without thinking), compulsivity (acting without caring whether actions will be harmful), problems delaying gratification, and the desire to seek out new experiences. This desire for new experiences is also a personality trait associated with Internet addiction. Others include being drawn to mental stimulation, having difficulty coping with boredom, and being able to spend time alone without feeling isolated from others. Studies of teens have also shown that the more emotionally stable, extroverted, and loyal someone is, the less likely that person is to become addicted to the Internet, probably because such people prefer face-to-face interactions over online ones.

Situational Causes

Other studies of high school students' Internet use found that loneliness is often a reason for Internet addiction. This is known as a situational cause because the addiction is driven by the cir-

Loneliness leads some high school students to develop addictive online habits like checking texts and social media sites all through the night. Life-changing or overwhelming events can have a similar effect.

cumstances in a person's life at the time the addiction takes hold. Addiction experts Kimberly Young, Xiao Dong Yue, and Li Ying have identified other situations that can lead to addiction. These include times when people are overwhelmed, experiencing personal problems, and/or are going through a life-changing event. Of these times, they say,

> the Internet can become a psychological escape that distracts a user from a real-life problem or difficult situation. For instance, someone going through a painful divorce can turn to online friends to help cope with the situation. For someone who has recently been relocated . . . starting over can be lonely. As a means to cope with the loneliness experienced by the new surroundings, a user can turn to the Internet to fill the void of those lonely evenings.[24]

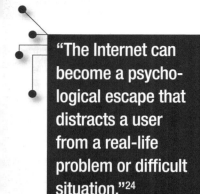
Periods of stress, anxiety, or depression can also play a role in the development of an Internet addiction. Young reports that on-line games are particularly good at attracting people who seek relief from the anxieties and stresses associated with everyday life. She says that such games "become a kind of es-cape mechanism for a lot of people."[25] Those with depression can similarly be drawn to the Internet as a way to distract themselves from their problems and to alter their mood.

Cross Addiction

A desire to avoid using drugs and alcohol is another form of escap-ism associated with addictive Internet use. "The [heavy Internet] user may also suffer from a history of alcohol or drug dependency, only to find in compulsive use of the Internet a physically safe alter-native to their addictive tendency," explain Young, Yue, and Ying. "They believe that being addicted to the Internet is medically safer than being addicted to drugs or alcohol, yet the compulsive be-havior still avoids the unpleasant situation underlying addiction."[26] In other words, these individuals have simply traded one addiction for another, without working through the issues that caused them to become addicts in the first place.

This tendency to substitute one addiction for another means that a main cause of an Internet addiction may be another addic-tion. As Young, Yue, and Ying report,

> Users who suffer from multiple addictions are at the great-est risk to suffer from Internet addiction. People who have addictive personalities may be more likely to use alcohol, cigarettes, drugs, food, or sex as a way of dealing with problems. They have learned to cope with situational diffi-culties through addictive behavior, and the Internet seems a convenient, legal, and physically safe distraction from those real-life problems.[27]

Cat Videos

Studies suggest that some people become addicted to the Internet because it gives them a way to turn a bad mood into a good one. Indeed, certain kinds of online content can elevate people's moods. For example, a 2015 study by Indiana University Media School researcher Jessica Gall Myrick found that viewing cat videos boosts energy and positive emotions and reduces negative emotions—particularly anxiety, annoyance, and sadness. Of her work, Myrick says, "Some people may think watching online cat videos isn't a serious enough topic for academic research, but the fact is that it's one of the most popular uses of the Internet today. If we want to better understand the effects the Internet may have on us as individuals and on society, then researchers can't ignore Internet cats anymore."

Quoted in IU Bloomington Newsroom, "Not So Guilty Pleasure: Viewing Cat Videos Boosts Energy and Positive Emotions, IU Study Finds," June 16, 2015. http://news.indiana.edu.

Indeed, various studies indicate that a majority of Internet addicts have one or more additional addictions. For example, one study by researchers in Greece, reported in 2012 in the *Journal of Internet Addiction*, found that the more heavily a teen used the Internet, the more likely the teen was to be addicted to drugs. Consequently, the researchers concluded that Internet addiction can be considered a predictor of substance abuse.

But Internet addictions can also exist all on their own, with no connection to other addictive behavior. As Elias Aboujaoude, assistant director of the Stanford School of Medicine's Obsessive-Compulsive Disorder Clinic, says, "From a clinical experience, I've seen plenty of people whose primary problem is an Internet problem. They're not gamblers, they're not pornography addicts, they're not necessarily depressed."[28] Such individuals might have what could be considered an addictive personality yet only lack self-control when it comes to Internet use.

Genetics

In cases where the Internet is the only addiction and no situational factors appear to have caused it, some experts believe that genetics may be involved. Found in every cell in the body, genes are essentially inherited instructions that provide a blueprint for an individual's physical characteristics and behavior. Their influence can be seen by comparing the traits of children in families who share the exact same genes (identical twins), some of the same genes (fraternal twins and other siblings), or none of the same genes (as when children are adopted into a family with existing children).

Research suggests that genes are responsible for roughly half of a person's chance of abusing substances like alcohol or marijuana. No one gene is responsible for substance abuse, but individual genes can contribute traits that seem to make a person more likely to become addicted to one particular substance

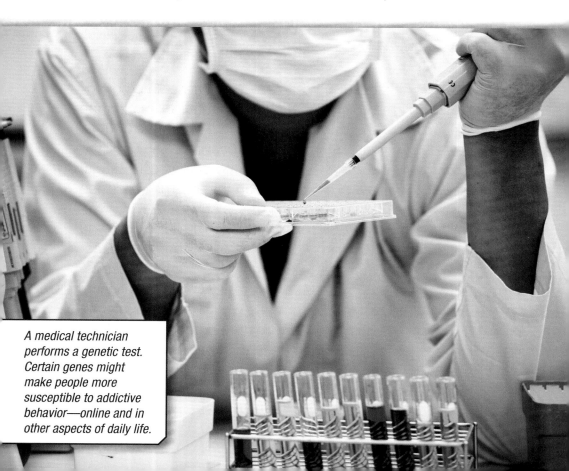

A medical technician performs a genetic test. Certain genes might make people more susceptible to addictive behavior—online and in other aspects of daily life.

or another. For example, a variant of the gene AKT1 appears to make people more susceptible to the mind-altering effects of THC (tetrahydrocannabinol), the active ingredient in cannabis, or marijuana. Similarly, a variant of the gene CHRNA5 appears to increase a person's susceptibility to nicotine, the active ingredient in cigarettes.

Research into family patterns supports the connection between heredity and addiction. In particular, identical twins are more likely to share an alcohol or nicotine addiction than fraternal twins are. The same is true of identical twins who have a gambling addiction. This suggests that behavioral addictions and substance addictions can have a genetic component.

> "Internet addiction is not a figment of our imagination."[29]
>
> —Molecular psychologist Christian Montag, who has studied the genes related to addiction.

This connection might have been confirmed by researchers from the University of Bonn in Germany, who announced in the September 2012 issue of the *Journal of Addiction Medicine* that they had found a gene associated with Internet addiction. Their study looked at a group of 132 individuals who reported having trouble staying away from the Internet and compared them with 132 individuals who reported having no such trouble. Researchers found that many of the individuals who considered themselves Internet addicts—especially the women—had a gene that the people in the nonaddicted group lacked: a variant of a gene known as CHRNA4.

Since other variants of CHRNA4 change brain chemistry in ways that appear to make people more susceptible to nicotine addiction, the lead author of the study, Christian Montag, is excited about the findings. He says that while more research is needed, "Internet addiction is not a figment of our imagination. The current data already shows that there are clear indications for genetic causes of Internet addiction."[29]

A Habit, Not an Addiction

However, others have cast doubt on the significance of Montag's study. For example, journalist Robert Wright realized that when

Anhedonia

Studies show that people who restlessly switch from one website to another are far more likely to develop symptoms of depression. Researchers do not yet know why this is the case. However, many suspect that at least some of the people who engage in such behavior are suffering from anhedonia, which is also associated with depression. Anhedonia involves a decreased ability to experience pleasurable emotions, but experts disagree on whether this is because the sufferer is unable to experience them or because the sufferer experiences these emotions but cannot make them last. In either case, an Internet addict who continually switches from website to website might be engaged in a desperate search for emotional stimulation.

the results were reported in the mainstream media, there was information that a variant gene had been identified, but no information on exactly how many of the people in Montag's study had it. After looking into this issue, Wright discovered that the results were not as impressive as they initially sounded. "The numbers are underwhelming," he says. Specifically, only 27 percent of the so-called addicts had the gene, and 17 percent of the nonaddicts also had it. He adds that "the chances that a non-addict will have the gene are, relatively speaking, pretty high—63 percent as high as the chances that an addict will have it."[30] In other words, there seemed to be a weak connection between having the variant gene and actually having an online addiction.

Wright acknowledges that further research might show Montag's work to be significant. But he currently believes that what many people deem an Internet addiction is simply a habit that has reached a dysfunctional level—which is slightly different than true addiction. His belief is based on the way that the body encourages people to develop habits. "Human beings are biochemical machines 'designed' by natural selection to, among other things, form habits," he explains. "In particular, we're designed to form habits that helped our ancestors survive and get genes into the next generation—such habits as eating meat or fruit or having sex with auspicious mates or impressing people or even gathering tactically useful information about people (i.e., gossip)."[31] Given that all people possess this pleasure-based mechanism for forming habits, Wright suggests that everyone, regardless of his or her genetic makeup, has the potential to become addicted to the Internet. Indeed, many individuals simply crave the rush of excitement and pleasure they get from going online. To them, the Internet is a fun diversion. Consequently, they are eager to use it, and as they rack up more and more pleasurable online experiences, they want to spend more and more time online.

Designed to Be Addictive

Some who share this view say it explains why marketing experts seem able to design apps and websites in ways that intentionally encourage people to become addicted to them. Jeremy Vandehey, who has created addictive apps for smartphones, says of his work, "We (as app makers) want them to be addicting. Like a potato chip manufacturer, we try to put just the right crunch and the perfect amount of salt so you can't help but have *just one more*. We want you to get addicted. It puts the potato chips on our table."[32]

One famously addictive app is the game *Candy Crush Saga,* which requires players to match up types of candies (by color, for example, or by whether they are striped or wrapped) as they progress through more than two thousand levels of play (to which more levels are continually added). While trying to win a level, players only get five chances, or lives, before they are locked out

> "We (as app makers) want them to be addicting. Like a potato chip manufacturer, we try to put just the right crunch and the perfect amount of salt so you can't help but have *just one more*."[32]
>
> —App creator Jeremy Vandehey.

of playing again until the lives are replenished (it takes about thirty minutes to earn back a life). In other words, players must wait thirty minutes before being able to play again, and when they do so they start with just one life—it takes two and a half hours to refresh all five lives.

Within a year of its April 2012 release on Facebook, *Candy Crush* had over 132 million players each month, and over 600 million gaming sessions each day on mobile devices alone. This amount of play is reflective of *Candy Crush*'s highly addictive nature. Experts have identified several reasons why the game is so addictive, including the fact that it is continually updated, that people can play with or compete against friends, and that the game provides a feeling of accomplishment.

A player enjoys a game of Candy Crush Saga. *Experts say this game is highly addictive because it continually updates, it allows competition with friends, and players feel a sense of accomplishment when they are done.*

Candy Crush is also appealing because, at first, it fits seamlessly into people's existing daily routine. Psychologist Jamie Madigan, who has studied the psychology of gaming, explains: "Candy Crush Saga is designed to be a habit, not a game." Madigan says that habits often grow out of routines, so games that are designed to fit into a person's daily routine have a better chance of becoming habit-forming, or addictive. "If you pick the game up over your morning coffee every day, or play on your lunch break, or play as part of your getting ready for bed routine," says Madigan, "it will become a habit."[33]

Ironically, *Candy Crush*'s limit on lives, which could simply force players to take occasional time-outs, only makes people even more addicted to the game. As one player, twenty-two-year-old Andy Jarc, explains, "'You always want what you can't have.' I can't have more lives and I want them."[34] People can buy additional lives, which both drives and reflects their addictive behavior.

Variant Rewards

Selling lives is just one way that apps and other companies profit from people's online addictions. Some companies earn money every time an Internet user views a webpage or clicks on a link. For example, if a website displays an ad for a product offered by the online merchant Amazon, a click on that ad—which results in the user being taken to the product's Amazon page—earns the website a 4 to 10 percent commission from Amazon on the resulting purchase.

Given how lucrative such transactions can be, companies have teams of specialists working on ways to make people view more webpages and interact more with each one. Many of these specialists' methods are based on the work of behavioral psychologist B.F. Skinner, particularly his studies in the 1930s and 1940s on reward-motivated behavior in pigeons and rats. For these studies, each animal was placed in a box that contained either a Plexiglas disk (for the pigeons) or a lever (for the rats). When pecked or pressed, respectively, this trigger would release food through an opening in the box wall, and over time the animal came to expect a reward every time the disk or lever was touched.

Then Skinner changed his system to one of variant reward. This meant that rewards were paid out randomly, irrespective of how many times the disk or lever was pecked or pressed in between each payout. Sometimes the reward payouts stopped for a few seconds, sometimes for a few minutes—but in either case, the animal continued to try to trigger the rewards through frantic, obsessive, excessive behavior. One pigeon, for example, pecked the disk eighty-seven thousand times over a sixteen-hour period even though the action paid off only 1 percent of the time.

Human beings exhibit the same behavior when in situations with variant rewards. This is why, for example, a person will sit for hours pulling the lever of a slot machine even though the payout is highly infrequent. It is also why people will keep checking for new e-mails or new online news alerts every few minutes. Each time they check (the equivalent of pressing a lever), they hope to be rewarded with a new message. Variant rewards can explain addictions to social media and Internet browsing as well. Here the trigger is something that catches the eye, and the action akin to pressing a lever is scrolling down and/ or clicking to view content that might be a reward in the form of an enjoyable article or video.

> "It's important to realise that many websites and other digital tools have been engineered specifically to elicit compulsive behaviour."[35]
>
> —Journalist Michael Schulson.

Manipulated into an Addiction

Since these features were created specifically to get people hooked on certain aspects of the Internet, some experts believe that most of the blame for online addiction lies with those in the field of Internet design who have worked to manipulate human behavior to their advantage. Journalist Michael Schulson, who often writes on issues related to technology and ethics, is one such expert. "Should individuals be blamed for having poor self-control?" he asks. "To a point, yes. Personal responsibility matters. But it's important to realise that many websites and other digital tools have been engineered specifically to elicit compulsive behaviour."[35]

In fact, Schulson says that tech companies employ teams of experts who know how to design apps, websites, and other Internet features in ways that will wear down someone's ability to resist going online. Schulson notes that when it comes to a battle between such experts and the willpower of someone who's already struggling with situational factors and personality traits that make addiction more likely, "it's not exactly a fair fight."[36]

CHAPTER THREE

The Physical Consequences of Online Addiction

Internet addicts can suffer from the same physical problems as anyone who leads a sedentary lifestyle. Remaining relatively motionless—except for busy fingers and thumbs— for long periods of time can result not only in a lack of fitness but in obesity and obesity-related ailments as well. In fact, a 2012 study by the Milken Institute, an independent think tank that supports a variety of research projects, found that every 10 percent rise in a country's expenditures on information and communications technology is accompanied by a 1 percent increase in obesity rates. But Internet addiction also brings physical consequences that do not stem simply from being sedentary.

Facebook Brain

Among the most concerning physical effects of online addictions are changes to the human brain. Researchers have used a type of scan known as magnetic resonance imaging (MRI) to look at the brains of Internet addicts and compare them to the brains of non-addicts. They have found several differences between the two. For example, a 2015 study out of the California State University Fullerton (CSUF) that employed MRIs to examine the brains of Facebook addicts found that two brain regions associated with causing impulsive behavior displayed more activity than normal. In other words, the Facebook users might have been stimulated to engage in addictive behavior.

A similar increased level of activity has been found in the brains of drug addicts as well, but typically in a different part of the brain. Based on this difference, researchers believe that while both drug addicts and Facebook users might have a physical reason why they feel compelled to engage in certain detrimental behaviors over and over again, only drug addicts appear to have a physical reason why they cannot stop themselves from doing so. According to the lead author of the study, psychologist Ofir Turel, Facebook addicts therefore "have the ability to control their behavior, but they don't have the motivation to control this behavior because they don't see the consequences to be that severe."[37] However, others note that it is unclear whether online addiction causes a Facebook user's brain to be this way or whether such brains are different to begin with.

Turel's study also found that people with so-called Facebook brain responded differently to visual cues related to Facebook. Specifically, when these addicts were shown various images that were a random mix of Facebook logos and traffic signs, they responded to the Facebook images—by pressing a button—much more quickly than they responded to the traffic signs. As a result, Turel says, someone driving a car who is also a Facebook addict is "going to respond faster to beeps from their cellphone [i.e., from the Facebook app] than to street signs."[38] Perhaps this is why various surveys have shown that roughly 10 percent of college-age drivers often or always respond to their smartphone's mobile apps while driving and one-third sometimes use the apps while driving.

Brain Damage?

Other studies have found that Internet addiction appears to alter certain areas of gray matter and white matter, two types of brain tissue associated with the central nervous system. Specifically, the gray matter in certain parts of the brains of Internet addicts can shrink as much as 10 to 20 percent, and the white matter can display abnormalities in density. In either case, the longer the person has been an Internet addict, the more pronounced these changes are.

The brain areas that have displayed gray matter shrinkage are responsible for such things as impulse control, prioritizing tasks, empathy, and compassion. The areas that have displayed white matter abnormalities are associated with memory formation and retrieval, executive function (a set of skills that helps people get

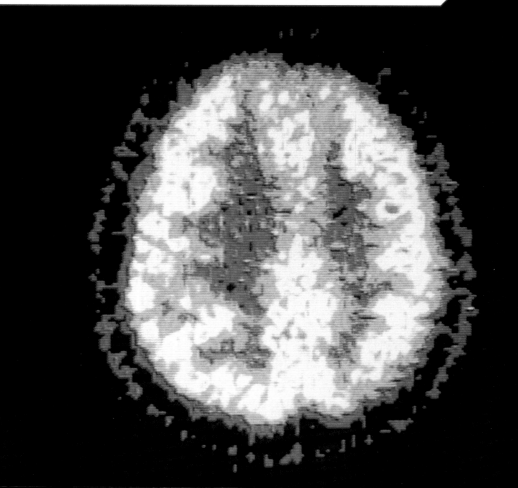

A scan shows gray matter (yellow and red coloring) and white matter (green and blue coloring) in a normal human brain. Some studies suggest that Internet addiction alters certain areas of the brain's gray matter and white matter.

things done, like prioritizing tasks), and cognitive function (learning, understanding, and applying information). White matter abnormalities have also been noted in brain areas involved in how certain parts of the brain communicate with other parts of the brain, particularly in regard to emotions, self-control, and decision making.

Some experts believe that the changes seen in the brains of Internet addicts should be considered brain damage. For example, child psychiatrist Victoria L. Dunckley says that too much time online "appears to impair brain structure and function." She is particularly concerned about the location of this impairment. "Much of the damage occurs in the brain's frontal lobe, which undergoes massive changes from puberty until the mid-twenties," she says. "Frontal lobe development, in turn, largely determines success in every area of life—from sense of well-being to academic or career success to relationship skills."[39]

But others believe that the brain abnormalities in online addicts are simply a reflection of a brain becoming specialized for a certain task. As an example, neuroscientist Karl Friston of University College London points to the fact that people who spend a lot of time playing an online game not only exhibit the type of brain changes seen in other kinds of Internet addicts but also become much better at the game over time. He says, "Our brains grow wildly until our early teens, then we start pruning and toning areas to work more efficiently. So these areas may just be relevant to being a good online gamer, and were optimized for that."[40]

To support his position, Friston cites a study that compared the brains of taxi drivers with those of bus drivers in London. The bus drivers always drove the same routes, whereas the taxi drivers had to learn and remember countless streets and locations. Probably not coincidentally, the taxi drivers' brains had denser gray matter in a part of the brain associated with navigation and memory.

The Brain, Rewired

Studies have also shown that certain online activities—such as ones that involve being rewarded with a prize (as in an online game) or with new content (as when checking for e-mails)—can stimulate brain neurons, which are cells that transmit nerve impulses, to release a chemical substance called dopamine into brain regions associated with pleasure. As a result, the activity that caused the dopamine release becomes associated with pleasure. Since the same process is seen in people addicted to substances like cocaine and nicotine, experts believe that dopamine-caused perceptions of pleasure are what drive people to seek out a particular online activity over and over again.

Researchers further believe that habitual reward-based activities can alter the brain in ways that cause it to crave more and more dopamine. This appears to have been the case, for example, with mice trained to press a lever to get a treat as part of a January 2016 study out of Duke University in North Carolina. Over time, a region of the rodents' brains that deals with reward and motivation was essentially rewired. Given such findings, some experts are concerned that the brains of people who engage in reward-based online activities are being similarly rewired. In fact, neuroscientist Nora Volkow of the National Institute on Drug Abuse notes, "I'd be surprised if playing online games for 10 to 12 hours a day didn't change the brain."[41]

> "I'd be surprised if playing online games for 10 to 12 hours a day didn't change the brain."[41]
>
> —Neuroscientist Nora Volkow of the National Institute on Drug Abuse.

Internet Use and ADHD

But even if gamers' brains are being rewired—and again, experts disagree on whether this is the case—it is unclear whether these changes damage mental ability. Studies have shown that the cortex—the outer layer of the brain—is thinner than normal at the frontal lobe in teenage boys who are addicted to online gaming, and some of these boys have exhibited learning difficulties. But experts disagree on whether the thinner cortex is the reason why these boys tend to struggle in school. Perhaps boys who struggle in school are simply more likely to be drawn to playing online games.

The same is true regarding the issue of whether Internet addiction is associated with attention-deficit/hyperactivity disorder

Thumb Problems

Addictions to texting, gaming, or other activities performed on a smartphone or tablet can result in thumb pain and even serious thumb injuries. For example, in 2015 doctors in San Diego, California, reported in the *Journal of the American Medical Association* that a twenty-nine-year-old man had developed pain and loss of motion in his left thumb as a result of playing the game *Candy Crush Saga* all day on his smartphone for at least six weeks straight. Surgery revealed that he had torn a tendon in the thumb.

Physicians say this kind of injury, which is caused by repetitive stress on the thumb joint, is on the rise. Moreover, because of the way that muscles and tendons in the hand are attached to the thumb, pain and mobility problems can occur not only in the thumb but in the wrist, hand, and fingers as well. Consequently, sufferers often develop an inability to grip things.

(ADHD). This disorder makes people restless, easily bored, and often unable to concentrate. Experts estimate that at least 11 percent of children ages five to seventeen currently have the disorder, and at least 4 percent of adults. Moreover, diagnoses of ADHD among young people in the United States rose 43 percent between 2003 and 2011 (the last year the government agency responsible for keeping track of such figures measured ADHD). No one knows the underlying reason(s) for this dramatic rise, but some have noted that it corresponds with a rise in Internet use among young people.

Indeed, Internet use and ADHD seem to go hand in hand. The more a particular person uses the Internet, the more likely that person is to have ADHD. Consequently, some experts have suggested that the Internet either causes ADHD or encourages it to flourish, perhaps because of Internet users' tendency to jump back and forth between online activities, websites, and the like.

But here again, as psychologist and ADHD expert Peter Killeen notes, it is unknown "which way the arrow of causality flows."[42]

Texting While Driving

There is no doubt, however, about causation when it comes to drivers who send or receive texts while behind the wheel. People who are addicted to texting to the point where they are unable to stop even while driving can cause serious and often fatal injuries. According to the National Safety Council, people who text while driving are eight times more likely to be involved in a crash. Moreover, cell phone use while behind the wheel accounts for 27 percent of all motor vehicle accidents in the United States each year. Put another way, the Centers for Disease Control and Prevention reports that each day at least fifteen people are killed and more than twelve hundred are injured in crashes involving a distracted driver, with cell phone use being the number one cause of driver distraction.

As an example of such a crash, in July 2015 seventeen-year-old Carlee Bollig of Little Falls, Minnesota, was texting while driving when her three passengers, also teenagers, told her to stop texting because it wasn't safe. She told them to leave her alone, adding that she "didn't care if she crashed."[43] A few moments later she ran a red light and crashed into a minivan driven by fifty-four-year-old Charles Mauer, a father of three. Mauer and his youngest daughter, age ten, were severely injured and soon died. Two other passengers in Mauer's car and all three of Bollig's passengers were also injured but survived. In March 2016 Bollig was sentenced to four years' probation and two hundred forty hours of community service for her negligence.

Posting While Driving

Investigators examined Bollig's phone to learn more about what contributed to the crash. They found that right before impact, she paused texting in order to post something on Facebook. Indeed, posting to online social media while driving has increased right along with an increase in addiction to such media. Some of the resulting crashes have been horrific. For example, in March 2015

Most people today understand that texting while driving can lead to serious and often fatal crashes. Those who ignore this danger by continuing to text and drive may be exhibiting signs of addiction.

police charged thirty-four-year-old Kari Jo Milberg of Oak Grove Township, Wisconsin, with homicide for killing her eleven-year-old daughter and two of her five-year-old nieces because she was posting messages on Facebook while driving. Her last message was sent to the site just two minutes before she veered into an opposing lane, hit a truck head-on, and was thrown from the car.

A study sponsored by AT&T found that of the 70 percent of smartphone users who admit using their phones while driving, 40 percent post on social media while driving, 30 percent search the Internet, and 10 percent video chat. Other studies have shown that at least 15 percent take selfies while driving, as was the case with thirty-two-year-old Courtney Sanford while driving on an interstate highway in North Carolina. She used her phone to take a photo of herself and share it on Facebook along with the caption, "The happy song makes me HAPPY!" She then veered into oncoming traffic, crashed into a truck, and died. Lieutenant Chris Weisner, who was involved in the investigation of the crash, says, "In a matter of seconds, a life was over just so she could notify some friends that she was happy."[44]

Slow Reaction Times

As Bollig's story illustrates, communicating online while driving can cause drivers to fail to hit the brakes. This is because such distractions can slow reaction time, as has been demonstrated in numerous studies. One of the most significant of such studies—because it was the first one done under real driving conditions instead of a laboratory simulator—was conducted by the Texas A&M Transportation Institute in October 2011. It involved forty-two drivers ages sixteen to fifty-four who had to navigate a roughly 11-mile (18 km) test track that included a section lined with construction barrels. First the drivers completed the course without distractions. Then they drove the same track while sending and receiving text messages. During both trials they were supposed to stop whenever they spotted a flashing yellow light on the track, and the researchers measured how quickly they responded to this signal.

> "In a matter of seconds, a life was over just so she could notify some friends that she was happy."[44]
>
> —Police lieutenant Chris Weisner, referring to a crash caused by a Facebook posting.

By the end of the test, researchers had discovered that texting added three to four seconds to a driver's reaction time—if he or she managed to stop at all. While either reading or sending a text, a driver was eleven times more likely to drive right past the light, often not even noticing it. "Our findings suggest that

Taking a selfie, posting on social media sites, or searching the Internet—all while driving—are foolish and dangerous actions. And yet people do them, possibly because of an online addiction or obsession.

response times are even slower than what we originally thought," says study head Christine Yager. "Texting while driving basically doubles a driver's reaction time and makes the driver less able to respond to sudden roadway dangers."[45]

The texting drivers in the study also had much more trouble maintaining a constant speed and staying in their driving lane. Moreover, researchers noted that other than the construction barrels, the course contained no driving hazards; drivers only had

Petextrians

In 2015 the Government Highway Safety Association reported that the number of pedestrian deaths has began to rise after years of decline. The organization blamed this continuing increase largely on "petextrians," people who text while walking. Many of those who have been killed or injured by distracted walking are teens. Indeed, according to a 2014 report by Safe Kids Worldwide, 40 percent of US teens ages thirteen to eighteen have been hit or nearly hit by an automobile, bicycle, or motorcycle while walking. Other studies have shown that victims are more likely to have been using a smartphone when the accident happened.

to go in a straight line on level ground and without other traffic. Consequently, they likely would have done even worse under real-world driving conditions.

A Refusal to Quit

Experts say that similar studies need to be conducted on drivers using other features of the Internet because it appears that going online while driving is even more dangerous than texting. Researcher Lauren McCartney of the University of Alabama at Birmingham expresses particular concern about the use of mobile apps while driving. "The technology is evolving so rapidly that science hasn't caught up to looking at the effects that mobile app usage can have behind the wheel of a car," she says. "But something needs to be done because in psychological terms, Internet use involves substantial cognitive and visual distraction that exceeds talking or texting, making it much more dangerous."[46]

Despite such findings, many online addicts have no intention of giving up their habits of texting, posting, browsing, or using mobile apps while behind the wheel. Surveys indicate that nearly 80 percent of young people who text while driving believe they can do so safely. The 30 percent who say they post on Twitter "all the time"[47] while driving show the same lack of concern.

However, psychologists suggest that this lack of concern might be superficial. That is, online addicts might say they are not worried about their behavior when, in fact, they are worried but feel powerless to do anything about it. Given the physical changes that have been seen in the brains of online addicts, this feeling might be understandable. Still, experts say, it should not prevent addicts from taking steps to combat their addiction—even though the amount of effort needed to overcome such an addiction can be daunting.

"The technology is evolving so rapidly that science hasn't caught up to looking at the effects that mobile app usage can have behind the wheel of a car."[46]

—Researcher Lauren McCartney of the University of Alabama at Birmingham.

CHAPTER FOUR

Living with an Online Addiction

Online addictions not only have physical consequences but psychological and emotional ones as well. They alter lifestyles, suck up time perhaps better spent on other activities, and even destroy relationships, careers, and finances. They also cause addicts to feel bad about themselves for being unable to kick their habit.

A Daily Obsession

Many online addictions involve games, and certain ones are especially known for altering lifestyles to a dangerous or harmful point. These include *Minecraft, Angry Birds, Words with Friends,* and, of course, *Candy Crush.* Addicted players find themselves unable to stop thinking about the game, and many play it in all corners of their lives. "From the time I started playing it was just all I could think about," says Erickka Sy Savane, a mother of two from New Jersey, of her addiction to *Candy Crush.* "I was one of those people you see on the trains and in the grocery store lines playing—whenever I had a free moment. . . . I would sneak away to be by myself so I could play. Put them [the kids] to bed early, drop them off at school really quick—just kinda push them to the side. It was all-consuming."[48]

More complex games like *World of Warcraft (WoW)* often draw addicted players into long gaming sessions as opposed to ones snatched here and there during spare moments. Created in 2004, *WoW* is what gamers call a massively multiplayer online role-playing game (MMORPG), in which players take on the role of a particular character and interact with other players in a fantasy world. As of November 2015 the game had 5.5 million subscribers, which earned it the Guinness World Record for the most popular MMORPG.

According to addiction experts, *WoW* is also one of the most highly addictive games. Moreover, because it encourages long playing periods, many addicts neglect important aspects of daily life in order to play. For example, sixty-nine-year-old Patricia, who worked in a library, missed Christmas dinners and other family get-togethers and vacations so she could play *WoW* as much as twelve hours a day. At the time she was having health problems, as was her husband, and the game was a way for her to escape her troubles. "I wanted to shut out real life totally," she says. "I just wanted to climb in the game and stay there."[49]

> "From the time I started playing it was just all I could think about."[48]
>
> —*Candy Crush* addict Erickka Sy Savane.

For university English professor Ryan van Cleave, the attraction of the game was the way it made him feel about himself at a time when marriage and child rearing were causing him stress. As he later shared in a book about his experiences, which he wrote after kicking his *WoW* addiction, "Playing WoW makes me feel godlike. I have ultimate control and can do what I want with few real repercussions. The real world makes me feel impotent . . . a computer malfunction, a sobbing child, a suddenly dead cellphone battery—the littlest hitch in daily living feels profoundly disempowering."[50]

Eventually Van Cleave was devoting so much time to *WoW*—roughly sixty hours a week—that his teaching contract was not renewed, he developed health problems, and he became emotionally unstable. As a result, he writes, "My kids hate me. My wife is threatening (again) to leave me. I haven't written anything in countless months. I have no prospects for the next academic year. And I am perpetually exhausted from skipping sleep so I can play more Warcraft."[51]

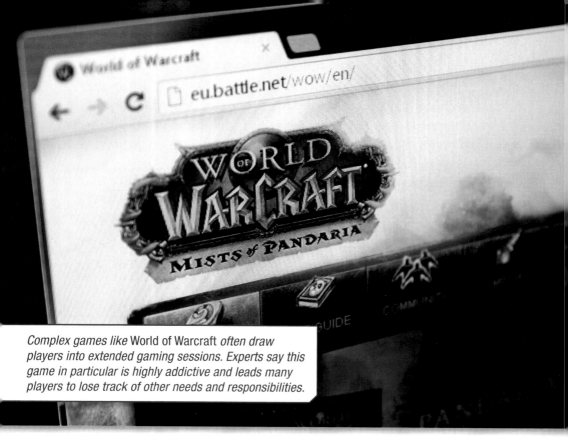

Complex games like World of Warcraft *often draw players into extended gaming sessions. Experts say this game in particular is highly addictive and leads many players to lose track of other needs and responsibilities.*

The Cost of Play

Van Cleave also spent a lot of money on his habit, not only because of the subscription fees he paid but also because he bought extra game features. For example, he spent $224 on virtual gold that his character could use to make weaponry purchases within the game. Van Cleave also bought two new computers so he could improve the graphics of his gaming experience.

Other games provide similar opportunities for players to drain their bank accounts. For example, *Candy Crush* offers players the chance to buy more lives, special candies, and other bonus features. *Candy Crush* designer Tommy Palm says that 70 percent of players reach the highest available level of game play without buying anything along the way, and studies of gaming on mobile devices suggest that only 1 percent of players spend money on extra game features. Nonetheless, that 1 percent spends billions of dollars on in-game purchases each year.

Gaming addicts spend hundreds per month on their habit. Megan Rose Dickey, for example, spent $127.41 on *Candy Crush* in just one week, buying not only extra lives but also special candies and other bonuses. Similarly, Ashley Feinberg, a writer for the website Gawker, spent $236 on the game before she realized she had a problem. She says that her buying habit started innocently enough. Failing to realize that she had used up all five of her lives, she hit the *try again* button and received a prompt asking if she wanted to buy a set of new lives for just ninety-nine cents. At that point she was close to completing a level—a level she had been stuck on for a week—and the cost seemed relatively insignificant. "You could easily lose that money in loose change doing laundry," she told herself. "What's the harm? What's one time?"[52]

But to her dismay, one time soon turned into many. As she reports, "I became a slave to the unstoppable force of Candy Crushing micropayments. It was so easy. It didn't even feel like I was spending money." But no matter how much she spent, she couldn't get herself to stop. "I always thought victory a mere swipe away," she says. "And the scariest part is that it didn't even take up that much time. Just in commuting both to and from work, I would have a good total hour in which I was free to crush candies, totally uninhibited by outside commitments and totally free to drop a good $10 easy."[53]

> "It was so easy. It didn't even feel like I was spending money."[53]
>
> —Ashley Feinberg, who spent $236 on *Candy Crush* extras.

The Cost to Relationships

Online addiction can also exact a price on romantic relationships since time spent on the Internet is usually time not spent with a spouse or partner. Sometimes the cost of such neglect is as minor as a little irritation, but cases of serious Internet addiction can lead to divorce. This is what happened to Ashley Yates (not her real name) of Salt Lake City, Utah, whose marriage ended because of her husband's *WoW* addiction. His habit began three weeks after their wedding. At first he played just a few hours a day because he was taking premed classes, but soon he was skipping school

Addiction-Fueled Illegal Behavior

A 2014 study of high school students in North Carolina suggested that teens who are addicted to the Internet find it difficult to differentiate between legal and illegal behavior. The research team reported in the journal *Computers in Human Behavior* that there was a correlation between Internet addiction and digital piracy (stealing online content). More than 40 percent of the students studied had some degree of Internet addiction. In addition, these students were far more likely to have illegally downloaded software than those who were not addicted. Interestingly, however, addiction seemed to have no bearing on whether a student pirated music or movies.

so he could play every waking hour, and he barely slept. When he did sleep, it was usually in front of his computer. He also ate in front of the computer, and he stopped showering and changing his clothes. As a result, he failed all his classes and only talked to her when he wanted to tell her something about the characters in his game.

Their marriage soon fell apart. Ashley now says of her ex-husband's compulsion to play *WoW*, "I don't think he could have stopped if he wanted."[54] Indeed, Massachusetts Institute of Technology professor Sherry Turkle, an expert in technology addiction, says of individuals with such a severe case of Internet addiction, "People behave just as if they were under the grip of cocaine. They are sneaking away to get on Facebook and putting game time above relationships."

Parent-child relationships can also suffer because of such addictions. As Turkle points out, "When Mom's reading 'Harry Potter' to her kids with her right hand and scrolling through her email with her left, the family dynamic is going to suffer. They're really not giving kids their full attention."[55]

Children can also become online addicts. This was the case, for example, with a three-year-old who developed an addiction to the video-sharing website YouTube. "This wasn't something that I meant to happen," the girl's mother says. "It was a bit disturbing." She reports that one day she and her daughter were watching music videos on a tablet when the girl demanded to see more and more of them. Unhappy with the sometimes child-inappropriate content of these videos, the mother coaxed her daughter to watch children's videos instead. Her daughter then became hooked on these videos. "Once she has the tablet and has started watching You-Tube, I know that I'm in for a fight [if I try to get her to stop]," says the mother. "There was one tantrum that she had when I went to take it away after two hours of letting her watch, where she literally threw herself on top of the tablet so that I couldn't take it away."[56]

"When Mom's reading 'Harry Potter' to her kids with her right hand and scrolling through her email with her left, the family dynamic is going to suffer."[55]

—Massachusetts Institute of Technology professor Sherry Turkle, an expert on technology addiction.

Relationships can suffer when parents spend more time with their online devices than with their kids. Other family relationships can also be affected by addictive online behavior.

Internal Conflict

Another consequence of online addiction is the deep shame and guilt associated with the behavior. For example, after Breanne Saldivar of Austin, Texas, became addicted to viewing online pornography, she had trouble handling the guilt associated with her secret activity. She explains, "It tore me up on the inside that I could be talking to someone one moment and know this thing that's going on in my life. I started to isolate myself, because I hated what I was doing. I hated that I couldn't stop."[57]

Experts say guilt is so prevalent among Internet addicts that it is actually considered a sign that someone is addicted. That is, if someone who denies being addicted feels guilty for spending so much time online, they are probably addicted. Experts also say that this guilt can cause other psychological problems. For example, the Ashwood Recovery outpatient addiction treatment center in Boise, Idaho, describes this as "a deep guilt that can result in depression after a period of time. Unfortunately, that depression rarely drives the addict to seek treatment. Instead it usually results in an even more intense addiction to the technology that's causing the addiction because that's where the person experiences temporary relief."[58] The Ashwood Recovery center also reports that this guilt often causes addicts to lie about how much time they spend online. If someone notices and comments on their excessive Internet use, they can become defensive and perhaps hostile about it.

Anxiety, Distraction, and Lost Opportunities

Anxiety is another emotion common to online addicts. In part this is because people who are anxious often turn to the Internet as a way to lose themselves in activities that quiet their negative thoughts and emotions. But it is also because addicts typically feel anxious whenever they cannot access the Internet.

This was borne out by a 2015 study conducted by researchers with the University of Missouri, University of Oklahoma, and Indiana University, who found that smartphone addicts do poorly on mental tasks when they are separated from their phones. Test subjects, all of whom had iPhones on or near them, were told that the study was to test a new wireless blood pressure cuff. Each subject then had his or her blood pressure and heart rate measured while working on a word search puzzle.

After completing the puzzle, the subject was told that his or her cell phone had interfered with the wireless connection, so the process would have to be repeated. This time, the subject's phone was placed some distance away—and while the subject was completing the second puzzle, someone on the research team surreptitiously called the phone, which the subject could

Anxiety over not being connected to the Internet leads some people to hang on to their phones even while they sleep. This level of anxiety can be disruptive—both day and night.

Severe Cases of Online Addiction

At times, online addictions have had severe, even deadly consequences. For example, in 2012 an eighteen-year-old in Taiwan collapsed in an Internet café and subsequently died after playing an online game for two days straight without eating or drinking. In 2011 a three-year-old girl in Las Cruces, New Mexico, died of severe malnutrition and dehydration because her mother, twenty-eight-year-old Rebecca Colleen Christie, was too busy playing *World of Warcraft* to care for her—a case of dramatic neglect that ultimately led to a murder conviction. And in 2015 in Nantong, China, a nineteen-year-old Internet addict became so desperate to end his addiction that he hacked off his own hand. Surgeons were able to reattach it, but it will never be fully functional—and the teen will undoubtedly be emotionally scarred for life.

not answer. Subjects did significantly worse on their puzzles and experienced significantly more anxiety the second time around. Consequently, the study's lead author, Russell Clayton of the University of Missouri, says, "Our findings suggest that iPhone separation can negatively impact performance on mental tasks. Additionally, the results suggest that iPhones are capable of becoming an extension of our selves such that when separated, we experience a lessening of 'self' and a negative physiological state."[59]

App designer Jeremy Vandehey can relate to the anxiety that online addicts often feel when separated from their phones. After realizing that he could not have a conversation with someone without obsessively checking his phone, he decided to periodically turn it off as a way to reduce his dependence on the device. After cutting back on use, Vandehey began to think about all the things he had lost because of his dependence on the device. One was the opportunity to engage in critical thinking and connect socially with people he cares about. He explains:

Remember the glory days when you would spend an entire afternoon playfully arguing with a spouse, sibling, or friend about some trivial factual disagreement like which NFL team had the most Super Bowl wins? I do. My brother and I would spend entire afternoons having intense debates about the most Google-able, answerable topics. The truth is the answers never mattered as much as the conversation. It brought us closer. It taught us how to communicate. How to debate. Today that intense argument would have fizzled out in 2 minutes with Google having the final say.[60]

Deeper Problems

Vandehey was able to cut back on his smartphone use, but many others find themselves unable to do so. Experts say this inability reflects deeper problems. For example, addiction expert Paul Hokemeyer explains that obsessive, addictive smartphone use is a symptom of other behavioral, health, or personality issues with which a person may be struggling. "What happens is that people who are suffering from issues like depression, anxiety, trauma, and socially-challenging personalities self-medicate by reaching for things outside of themselves to manage their internal discomfort," says Hokemeyer. "Because technology plays such an integral part of our lives, smartphones easily become their object of choice."[61]

Experts also note that more and more people seem to be displaying this kind of behavior. As Charlotte Hilton Andersen, a writer with expertise in both psychology and computer information systems, notes, "We all know the girl who texts through dinner dates, compulsively checks Instagram to see what all her friends are eating at other restaurants, or ends every argument with a Google search—she's one of those people so tied to their cell phones that it's never out of arm's reach."[62] And perhaps because such behavior is so prevalent, many people view it as normal—but that does not make it any less harmful to those who are suffering from an Internet addiction.

CHAPTER FIVE

Breaking an Online Addiction

S ome people continue to struggle with their online addiction, either because they do not believe they have a problem or because they lack the will to address it. But others have attempted to break the devastating patterns that hold them hostage. In doing so, some rely on willpower to reduce or quit their use of mobile devices altogether. Others delete addictive apps from their devices in order to thwart temptation, or they look for help in the form of addiction-fighting apps.

Addiction-Fighting Apps

Addiction-fighting apps are specifically designed to help people have better self-control when it comes to Internet use. Many are designed to block access to the Internet as a whole and/or to certain sites and apps during certain time periods. For example, the Freedom app prevents users from going online for up to eight hours, blocking access to both websites and apps. The Anti-Social app automatically blocks the most common time-wasting sites—including Twitter, Facebook, Flickr, Digg, Reddit, YouTube, Hulu, Vimeo, and e-mail programs—for a set period of time.

Some apps allow users to override a blockage, but others make this impossible. An example of the latter is the Self-Control app, which blocks access to preset Internet sites during preset time periods and cannot be turned off once the restricted time period has started. Another blocking app, Procrastination Punisher, does allow the block to be removed—but only if the user pays a fee that will be donated to a preselected charity.

Other apps help users determine whether they have an Internet addiction and, if so, which Internet activities are most problematic for them. For example, FocusMe is a subscription service that not only blocks certain websites during preset focus sessions but also provides users with the option to track all their Internet and app activities to determine how much time they spend on each one. An app called TrackTime does this as well.

Parents of teen drivers have installed blocking apps to keep them from texting while driving. One such app is CellControl, which blocks access to preselected phone numbers and apps. A parent might choose, for example, to block a teen's ability to send texts, instant messages, and e-mails and to access social media sites while still allowing the teen to listen to music or hear navigational directions. CellControl can also provide parents with data regarding the driver's acceleration, braking, and speed.

Another approach to curtailing teen texting while driving is the Teen Driver Support System, which is under development at the HumanFIRST Laboratory in the Department of Mechanical Engineering of the University of Minnesota. This system relies on computer software within a small box that has been installed under a vehicle's driver's seat. When the car starts, the software syncs to the driver's phone via a Bluetooth wireless connection. This launches a preinstalled app that prevents the phone from doing anything except sending information to parents regarding their teen's driving habits, using data provided by various other features within the car. For example, seatbelt sensors tell parents whether the teen has buckled up, and sensors under the floorboards tell them whether other people are riding in the car.

Teens who try to disable the app so they can regain control of their phone—perhaps to text or access social media—will find they are unable to do so. "They can try, but it will come back,"

Even when there are consequences, many teens have difficulty putting their cell phones away during classes. Teachers say that students come up with all sorts of ways to circumvent the rules.

says Nichole Morris, a research associate at the lab. "They can try to open something else, and it's just going to pop up in front of it. I call it a 'zombie app', because you can't kill it."[63]

Phone Bans

Some experts have suggested applying this kind of technology to classrooms since smartphone use in schools has become a growing problem that hinders students' ability to learn. But education professionals point out that it is much simpler and cheaper to simply ban mobile phones from school grounds. Indeed, a 2012 study by the London School of Economics found that when such bans were enacted, teens' test scores rose by 6 percent.

But teachers report it can be extremely difficult to enforce such bans because teen Internet addicts disregard them and/or go to great lengths to circumvent them. This is true even when there are serious consequences for violating a smartphone ban. For example, a ban on bringing phones onto school property in the Garland Independent School District in Texas proved a failure, even though it required students caught with a phone to either pay fifteen dollars to get it back or to call a parent to come pick the phone up immediately. Consequently, the ban was lifted in favor of allowing students to use their phones at lunch, between classes, or in a classroom where a teacher has given them permission to do so.

This approach is becoming common in the United States, but some teachers do not like it. For example, Philip McIntosh, a science teacher in a Texas middle school, says, "It's no fun to constantly be hassling people about their cell phones. There's no joy in it." McIntosh does not allow students to use phones in his classroom at all, but he says that when he allowed their use on a limited basis it was even more of a hassle because of the students' attitudes. "They're so attached to those devices, it got to the point where they felt like it was their right and privilege to do whatever they wanted with it at any time, without any respect for what anybody else thought they should be doing."[64]

Going After Designers

Indeed, because of the nature of addiction, many Internet addicts are so concerned with satisfying their urges that they fail to consider the consequences of their actions. A student might not care whether using a smartphone in class interferes with his or her education or anyone else's, just as a driver who is anxious to send a text might not care whether it results in a ticket, a fine, or an accident.

Because bans that target addictive behavior can be ineffective, some technology experts have suggested targeting the creators of addictive activities instead. In particular, there have been calls to ban Internet designers from employing certain features of compulsive design into their apps and websites. Michael Schulson, who writes about issues related to technology, is among those who have suggested such a ban. He says, "The most obvious target here is continuous or infinite scroll. Right now, sites such as Facebook and Twitter automatically and continuously refresh the page. . . . YouTube, Netflix and similar sites automatically load the next video or show."[65] This makes it entirely too easy for people to keep reading or watching, which enables addictive behavior.

Another feature that encourages addiction is embedding links to other articles within articles. For example, an Internet user clicks on a headline for a breaking news story and starts reading it. A few paragraphs into the story are links to other articles that provide background information related to the news story. Within those articles are links to still more articles, some related, some not, along with enticing advertisements to click on for more information. This encourages endless web surfing in a way that some believe feeds addiction.

> "We could require companies to let the users decide how many deliveries of email they receive per day, or how often a social network can update their feeds."[66]
>
> —Writer Michael Schulson.

Schulson also argues that designers should be required to incorporate features into their apps and sites that reduce the chance that users will become addicted. "We could require companies to let the *users* decide how many deliveries of email they receive per day, or how often a social network can update their feeds," suggests Schulson. "Dashboards could also allow users to shape certain features of page layout, such as the amount of new content they see on a single page."[66]

Indeed, some people who work in tech are proponents of what is known as ethical design—Internet features that do not exploit users' addictive tendencies. Ethical design might involve a World

Life After Addiction

When she was using her smartphone from morning to night, and even overnight while she slept, Jenna Woginrich could barely imagine life without the device. But since getting rid of her phone and using only a landline and computer for Internet needs, her life has become much richer, more meaningful, and more enjoyable. She describes the social transformation she experienced upon kicking her device to the curb:

> I got a landline and I got more sleep. I look people in the eye. I eat food instead of photographing it and am not driving half a ton of metal into oncoming traffic while looking down at a tiny screen. My business, social life, and personal safety have not evaporated overnight either. Turns out a basic Internet connection and laptop is plenty of connectivity to keep friends informed, weekends fun and trains running on time. And while I might be missing out on being able to call 911 at any moment, it's worth the sacrifice to me. Alcoholics can clean wounds with 100 proof vodka, but that doesn't mean they should have it in their back pocket just in case.

Jenna Woginrich, "How I Quit My Smartphone Addiction and Really Started Living," *Guardian* (Manchester, UK), February 11, 2016. www.theguardian.com.

Wide Web that is much more flexible, wherein platforms and apps have time limits for use, hold the delivery of nonessential e-mails, or otherwise avoid constantly presenting the user with endless content.

Policing Addicts

Another suggestion for curbing online addiction is to have Internet providers monitor users for egregious or addictive behavior and flag them for it. Companies like Facebook and Twitter are already able to track the amount of time that users spend on their sites, and some people suggest they should use this data to prevent addiction. "If citizens wanted to do something [about Internet addiction]," says Schulson, "we could [compel] companies to provide cut-off points, and to alert users when their usage patterns resemble psychologically problematic behaviour."[67]

But other people are uncomfortable with the idea of policing people's online behavior, saying it threatens individual freedom. Computer programmer Paul Graham points out that one person's *excessive* is another person's *normal*, and learning how to deal with temptation is simply part of life. "Most people I know have problems with Internet addiction," says Graham. "We're all trying to figure out our own customs for getting free of it. That's why I don't have an iPhone, for example; the last thing I want is for the Internet to follow me out into the world."[68] Graham and others believe that responsibility for dealing with an Internet addiction rests primarily with the individual and not with companies or app designers.

> "Most people I know have problems with Internet addiction. We're all trying to figure out our own customs for getting free of it."[68]
>
> —Programmer Paul Graham.

Turning to Therapy

In their attempt to take responsibility for their problem, many online addicts have turned to therapy. Among the most successful type of therapy used to treat online addiction is cognitive behavioral therapy (CBT), which helps people identify problematic thought patterns and change them for the better. Patients explore the thoughts and feelings that trigger their behaviors and learn to recognize situations in which they are most likely to be tempted to engage in unwanted behavior.

For example, online shopping addict Kate Abbott, a stay-at-home mom, spent her first CBT session exploring the question of how she would feel if she couldn't shop online anymore. Abbott's answers led her to realize that her buying sprees, which cost $2,000 to $3,000 a month more than her family's income, occurred not because she really wanted particular items but because her purchases fulfilled certain emotional needs. These included "to reward myself after or before or during a long day of invisible parenting work. To reward [my son] Henry for putting up with me as an imperfect mother. To give Henry fun things to play with because I didn't always want to play with him myself."[69]

At the heart of these needs, Abbott says, was the feeling that "Henry and I both deserved stuff as a reward for getting through trying days, and that my personality and interests weren't entirely overcome by being an at-home mom. I didn't want to feel

Some people believe that social media companies, which track user time on their sites, could use this information to prevent addictive online behavior. Others warn that these companies should not be policing individual online behavior.

Asian Boot Camps

As of 2015, at least one in ten South Koreans between the ages of ten and nineteen were addicted to the Internet, many of them seriously. Consequently, the government has set up a network of boot camps (also known as rehab camps) designed to treat young people for their addiction. Lasting days or weeks, these camps offer a technology-free environment, opportunities to play sports and enjoy hobbies, and one-on-one counseling to teach them how to avoid becoming readdicted after going home.

But in China, which has roughly the same percent of Internet-addicted young people as South Korea, the boot camp experience is quite different. Lasting three to four months, these camps feature military-style physical training, medication, therapy sessions, and machines that monitor brain activity. Campers must wear camouflage uniforms and sleep in bare cells at night. They are guarded by soldiers who ensure they do not run away, access technology, or communicate privately with anyone from the outside world. In addition, some teens have been beaten while at camp, and in June 2014 a nineteen-year-old girl died after being kicked for two hours because she went to the bathroom without permission.

Addiction experts in other countries have condemned China's treatment methods while lauding South Korea's. However, those who run the Chinese boot camps claim that their approach is the one that gets the best results, insisting that their success rate is 75 percent (a claim that is unverifiable).

powerless. I had money, so I could spend it. And I did."[70] But over time, with the help of her therapist, Abbott learned to control her behavior. She also developed other interests and an identity outside of being a mother, channeling her energy into creative writing rather than shopping.

Treatment Centers

Abbott's counseling sessions took place in a therapist's office and were scheduled around the demands of her regular daily life. But some people seek out more intensive therapy, which is typically offered at treatment centers that specialize in helping addicts. For example, the Center for Internet and Technology Addiction in West Hartford, Connecticut, offers two- and five-day intensive outpatient treatment programs on Internet, gaming, personal device, and social media addictions.

Other centers offer programs that require patients to live at the center for a period of weeks or months, completely cut off from all access to technology. An example of this is reSTART, a Seattle-area rehab center that treats a variety of Internet and technology addictions. Inpatient treatment programs last seven to ten weeks, during which patients participate in therapy sessions and develop skills that help them cope with technological temptation once they leave the center. They also have access to activities that promote physical health, such as yoga, massage, and outdoor sports such as hiking and climbing.

Hilarie Cash, one of the founders of reSTART, says of the center's patients, "Our clinic treats only very serious cases. Most of the people that come are young adult males around the ages of 18 to 30 who spend a lot of time on the internet. Their health is poor, their social relationships have turned to crap, they have no social confidence or real-world friends. They don't date. They don't work."[71] Some of these people are so addicted that they have tremendous difficulty adjusting to therapy. Addiction counselor Tonya Camacho says that while working with Internet addicts in Peoria, Illinois, she encountered individuals who were incapable of going without Internet access even after being admitted to a facility designed to wean them off their devices. "They just can't live without it,"[72] she says. These people either smuggled smartphones or tablets into the facility so they could sneak onto the Internet or they walked out of the place, never to return.

Warning Labels

Because smartphones and tablets can be so addictive for certain individuals, some people argue that they should come with warning labels to let people know about the risk of developing an addiction. Among the first to propose warning labels was a group of psychologists and computer scientists from Bournemouth University in the United Kingdom in 2015. A leading member of this group, computer scientist Raian Ali, surveyed Internet users and found that 80 percent supported the idea of having warning labels on digital devices.

Ali says that the warning labels could be interactive, such as a message that pops up on the screen and requires the user to acknowledge it with a click. He believes that this would help people understand the dangers of becoming hooked on the Internet and help them alter their behavior accordingly. "Labels raise awareness and enable people to make a sort of self-monitoring so that they can adjust their usage style or at least take an informed decision about it," he says. "It is like having a scale at home to measure your weight and regulate your eating style."[73] His position is that it is easier to prevent an Internet addiction than to deal with an existing one, and many other experts—and addicts themselves—would likely agree with this assessment.

> "The hardest part of my day is walking through the computer lab [at school] to get to my English class."[74]
>
> —Ben, a recovering Internet addict.

The Struggle to Abandon Technology in an Increasingly Connected World

Some individuals will face a lifetime of temptation and struggle in their effort to maintain a healthy balance between online and offline activities, especially because the world is only getting more and more Internet enabled. Ben, who had a web-surfing addiction so serious that it caused him to flunk out of college and attempt suicide, benefited from group therapy sessions at the Illinois Insti-

Computers and cell phones are unquestionably essential tools of modern life. For this reason, they will continue to present challenges to those who struggle to find a healthy balance between online and offline activities.

tute for Addiction Recovery. Eventually he was able to go back to school, but Ben notes that he will always struggle with the urges that led him to develop the addiction in the first place, especially because the tools of addiction are all around him. "The hardest part of my day is walking through the computer lab [at school] to get to my English class,"[74] he says.

Indeed, even people who can do without their devices for a while, or for certain activities, typically cannot maintain a policy of staying away from technology forever because computers and the Internet are too integral a part of contemporary life. "You can't just pull the plug and expect to function," says columnist Maria Konnikova. "A student may be suffering from what she's

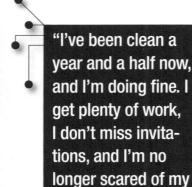

doing online, but she also might need to use the Internet for her classes. The thing she needs to avoid in order to do well is also the thing she needs to use to reach the same end."[75]

However, breaking an Internet addiction may be well worth the effort. Jenna Woginrich used to be consumed by an obsession to constantly check e-mails, update social media, play games, and listen to audiobooks via her smartphone. One day she realized she couldn't go a full minute without having the device in her hands. Consequently, she replaced her phone with a landline and reports that her life now feels richer, more meaningful, and more fulfilling. "I've been clean a year and a half now, and I'm doing fine. I get plenty of work, I don't miss invitations, and I'm no longer scared of my own thoughts."[76]

SOURCE NOTES

Introduction: From Pastime to Compulsion

1. Quoted in John D. Sutter, "How Smartphones Make Us Superhuman," CNN, September 10, 2012. www.cnn.com.
2. Quoted in Kristina Loring, "Teens Digitally Detox," KALW Radio, February 19, 2015. http://kalw.org.
3. Quoted in Katrina Schwartz, "What Happens When Teens Try to Disconnect from Tech for Three Days," KQED News, March 6, 2015. http://www.kqed.org.
4. Quoted in Sutter, "How Smartphones Make Us Superhuman."
5. Quoted in Jon Henley, "Teenagers and Technology: 'I'd Rather Give Up My Kidney than My Phone,'" *Guardian* (Manchester, UK), July 16, 2010. www.theguardian.com.
6. Ontogeny Partners, "Save Me from My iPad!," www.theontogenypartners.com.
7. Quoted in Lauren F. Friedman, "Why Internet Addiction Is So Hard to Stop," Business Insider, November 26, 2014. www.businessinsider.com.

Chapter One: The Nature of Online Addiction

8. Quoted in Clare Foran, "The Rise of the Internet-Addiction Industry," *Atlantic,* November 5, 2015. www.theatlantic.com.
9. Center for Internet Addiction, "FAQs: What Is Internet Addiction Disorder?" http://netaddiction.com.
10. Michael Murphy, "I'm Addicted to Online Gaming, and It Almost Ruined My Life," *Washington Post,* November 4, 2014. www.washingtonpost.com.
11. Center for Internet Addiction, "FAQs: What Is Internet Addiction Disorder?"
12. Tony Schwartz, "Addicted to Distraction," *New York Times,* November 28, 2015. www.nytimes.com.

13. Center for Internet Addiction, "FAQs: How Do You Know If You Have Internet Addiction (IA)?" http://netaddiction.com.
14. Schwartz, "Addicted to Distraction."
15. Center for Internet Addiction, "FAQs: Do Men and Women Differ in What They Become Addicted To?" http://netaddiction.com.
16. Maria Konnikova, "Is Internet Addiction a Real Thing?," *New Yorker,* November 26, 2014. www.newyorker.com.
17. Quoted in Konnikova, "Is Internet Addiction a Real Thing?"
18. Konnikova, "Is Internet Addiction a Real Thing?"
19. Danah Boyd, "Blame Society, Not the Screen Time," *New York Times,* July 16, 2015. www.nytimes.com.
20. Quoted in Baylor Media Communications, "'Cyberchondria'— Anxiety from Online Searches About Health—Is Worse for Those Who Fear the Unknown, Baylor Study Shows," October 7, 2013. www.baylor.edu.

Chapter Two: The Causes of Online Addiction
21. Konnikova, "Is Internet Addiction a Real Thing?"
22. Adrian F. Ward and Piercarlo Valdesolo, "What Internet Habits Say About Mental Health," *Scientific American,* August 14, 2012. www.scientificamerican.com.
23. Quoted in Marisa Cohen, "Do You Have an Addictive Personality?," WebMD. www.webmd.com.
24. Kimberly Young, Xiao Dong Yue, and Li Ying, "Prevalence Estimates and Etiologic Models of Internet Addiction," in *Internet Addiction: A Handbook and Guide to Evaluation and Treatment*, ed. Kimberly S. Young and Cristiano Nabuco de Abreu. New York: John Wiley & Sons, 2010, p. 13.
25. Quoted in Rheana Murray, "Cautionary Tales from People Obsessed with Candy Crush," ABC News, November 6, 2014. http://abcnews.go.com.
26. Young, Yue, and Ying, "Prevalence Estimates and Etiologic Models of Internet Addiction."
27. Young, Yue, and Ying, "Prevalence Estimates and Etiologic Models of Internet Addiction."
28. Quoted in Benny Evangelista, "Internet Addiction Can Harm Real Relationships," *San Francisco Chronicle*, November 15, 2009. www.sfgate.com.

29. Quoted in Elizabeth Armstrong Moore, "Internet Addiction Fueled by Gene Mutation, Scientists Say," CNET, August 29, 2012. www.cnet.com.

30. Robert Wright, "Do You Have the 'Internet-Addiction Gene'?," *Atlantic,* September 4, 2012. www.theatlantic.com.

31. Quoted in Daniel Lende, "Debating Addiction and Evolutionary Psychology on Bloggingheads," *Neuroanthropology* (blog), October 15, 2012. http://blogs.plos.org.

32. Jeremy Vandehey, "This Is Your Brain on Mobile," *Medium* (blog), April 10, 2014. https://medium.com.

33. Quoted in Jennifer Van Grove, "Candy Crush: You Play, You're Hooked. Now What?," CNET, September 2, 2013. www.cnet.com.

34. Quoted in Eliana Dockterman, "*Candy Crush Saga*: The Science Behind Our Addiction," *Time*, November 15, 2013. http://business.time.com.

35. Michael Schulson, "User Behavior," Aeon, November 24, 2015. https://aeon.co.

36. Schulson, "User Behavior."

Chapter Three: The Physical Consequences of Online Addiction

37. Quoted in Tia Ghose, "What Facebook Addiction Looks Like in the Brain," LiveScience, January 27, 2015. www.livescience.com.

38. Quoted in Ghose, "What Facebook Addiction Looks Like in the Brain."

39. Quoted in Victoria L. Dunckley, "Gray Matters: Too Much Screen Time Damages the Brain," *Mental Wealth* (blog), *Psychology Today,* February 27, 2014. www.psychologytoday.com.

40. Quoted in Dave Mosher, "High Wired: Does Addictive Internet Use Restructure the Brain?," *Scientific American,* June 17, 2011. www.scientificamerican.com.

41. Quoted in Mosher, "High Wired."

42. Quoted in Caitlin Dewey, "Is the Internet Giving Us All ADHD?," *Washington Post*, March 25, 2015. www.washingtonpost.com.

43. Quoted in AOL News, "Teen Kills 10-Year-Old Girl and Father of 3 While Texting and Driving," October 20, 2015. www.aol .com.
44. Quoted in Lindsey Eaton, "Woman Posts About 'Happy' Song on Facebook Seconds Before Fatal Business 85 Crash," Fox 8 News, April 25, 2014. http://myfox8.com.
45. Quoted in North America News, "Texas Texting Study Finds Driver Reaction Times Slower than Previously Thought," January 2012. www.alertdriving.com.
46. Quoted in Remy Melina, "35% of College Students Use Mobile Apps While Driving," LiveScience, June 27, 2011. www .livescience.com.
47. Quoted in Matt Richtel, "Some People Do More than Text While Driving," *Bits* (blog), *New York Times,* May 19, 2015. http://bits.blogs.nytimes.com.

Chapter Four: Living with an Online Addiction

48. Quoted in Rheana Murray, "Cautionary Tales from People Obsessed with Candy Crush," ABC News, November 6, 2014. http://abcnews.go.com.
49. Quoted in Cecilia D'Anastasio, "Inside the Tragic, Obsessive World of Video Game Addicts," *Vice,* January 26, 2015. www.vice.com.
50. Quoted in Tamara Lush, "At War with World of Warcraft: An Addict Tells His Story," *Guardian* (Manchester, UK), August 29, 2011. www.theguardian.com.
51. Quoted in Lush, "At War with World of Warcraft."
52. Ashley Feinberg, "Holy Shit I Just Spent $236 on Candy Crush, Help," Gizmodo, August 7, 2013. http://gizmodo.com.
53. Feinberg, "Holy Shit I Just Spent $236 on Candy Crush, Help."
54. Quoted in Elizabeth Stuart, "Internet Addiction Harming Marriage," *Deseret News* (Salt Lake City, UT), July 20, 2011. www.deseretnews.com.
55. Quoted in Stuart, "Internet Addiction Harming Marriage."
56. *Digital Parenting Blog,* "A Day with a Child Addicted to YouTube," January 22, 2015. http://yourekavach.com.
57. Quoted in John Donvan and Mary-Rose Abraham, "Is the Internet Driving Pornography Addiction Among School-Aged Kids?," ABC News, May 8, 2012. http://abcnews.go.com.
58. Ashwood Recovery, "Signs You Have a Technology Addiction." https://ashwoodrecovery.com.

59. Quoted in Gary Thayer, "Study: Smartphone Addiction Withdrawal Is Physical, Mental," Mobile Village, February 20, 2015. www.mobilevillage.com.

60. Vandehey, "This Is Your Brain on Mobile."

61. Quoted in Charlotte Hilton Andersen, "Cell Phone Addiction Is So Real People Are Going to Rehab for It," *Shape,* May 11, 2015. www.shape.com.

62. Andersen, "Cell Phone Addiction Is So Real People Are Going to Rehab for It."

Chapter Five: Breaking an Online Addiction

63. Quoted in Danielle Wong, "A Smartphone App for Teen Drivers: U of M Developing Teen Driver Support System to Keep Teens Safe on the Road," ThreeSixty, May 15, 2015. http://threesixtyjournalism.org.

64. Quoted in Dian Schaffhauser, "Are Cell Phone Bans Worth the Trouble?," *THE Journal*, October 20, 2014. https://thejournal.com.

65. Schulson, "User Behavior."

66. Schulson, "User Behavior."

67. Schulson, "User Behavior."

68. Paul Graham, "The Acceleration of Addictiveness," July 2010. www.paulgraham.com.

69. Kate Abbott, "The Responsible Thief," Billfold, May 1, 2012. https://thebillfold.com.

70. Abbott, "The Responsible Thief."

71. Quoted in Ned Hepburn, "Life in the Age of Internet Addiction," *Week*, January 24, 2013. http://theweek.com.

72. Quoted in Amy Jacobson and Emily Friedman, "Can't Stop Web Surfing? Go to Rehab," ABC News, August 7, 2008. http://abcnews.go.com.

73. Quoted in Carolyn Gregoire, "Psychologists Push for Smartphone Warning Labels," *Huffington Post*, October 8, 2015. www.huffingtonpost.com.

74. Quoted in Jacobson and Friedman, "Can't Stop Web Surfing?"

75. Konnikova, "Is Internet Addiction a Real Thing?"

76. Jenna Woginrich, "How I Quit My Smartphone Addiction and Really Started Living," *Guardian* (Manchester, UK), February 11, 2016. www.theguardian.com.

American Psychiatric Association (APA)

1000 Wilson Blvd., Suite 1825
Arlington, VA 22209
phone: (703) 907-7300; toll-free: (888) 357-7924
e-mail: apa@psych.org
website: www.psych.org

Established in 1844, the APA is the world's largest psychiatric organization, representing more than thirty-three thousand psychiatric physicians worldwide. Its website provides information about mental health issues and APA publications.

Center for Internet Addiction

PO Box 72
Bradford, PA 16701
phone: (814) 451-2405
website: www.netaddiction.com

The Center for Internet Addiction offers counseling for problematic Internet use and related issues. Its website provides information on issues such as compulsive web surfing and online gambling.

Center for Internet and Technology Addiction

17 S. Highland St.
West Hartford, CT 06119
phone: (860) 561-8727
e-mail: drdave@virtual-addiction.com
website: www.virtual-addiction.com

The Center for Internet and Technology Addiction provides counseling, information, and resources related to online addictions. Its website offers articles, news releases, and videos related to these addictions.

Illinois Institute for Addiction Recovery

5409 N. Knoxville Ave.
Peoria, IL 61614
phone: (800) 522-3784
website: www.addictionrecov.org

The Illinois Institute for Addiction Recovery provides treatment for all forms of addiction, including Internet and gaming addictions. Its website offers information related to these issues and provides access to the institute's online magazine, *Paradigm*, which contains articles for professionals and individuals interested in addiction-related subjects.

On-Line Gamers Anonymous (OGA)

PO Box 67
Osceola, WI 54020
phone: (612) 245-1115
website: www.olganon.org

The OGA is a fellowship group for compulsive gamers that also offers support for the loved ones of people suffering from a gaming addiction.

reSTART Internet and Technology Addiction Recovery

1001 290th Ave. SE
Fall City, WA 98024-7403
phone: (800) 682-6934
e-mail: contactus@netaddictionrecovery.com
website: www.netaddictionrecovery.com

reSTART is a Washington State inpatient treatment center for Internet addicts. The center's website offers information about online addiction and related problems.

Books

Danah Boyd, *It's Complicated: The Social Lives of Networked Teens*. New Haven, CT: Yale University Press, 2014.

Nicholas Carr, *The Glass Cage: How Our Computers Are Changing Us*. New York: W.W. Norton, 2015.

Nicholas Carr, *The Shallows: What the Internet Is Doing to Our Brains.* New York: W.W. Norton, 2010.

Howard Gardner and Katie Davis, *The App Generation: How Today's Youth Navigate Identity, Intimacy, and Imagination in a Digital World*. New Haven, CT: Yale University Press, 2013.

Samuel McQuade et al., *Internet Addiction and Online Gaming*. New York: Chelsea House, 2012.

Andrea Nakaya, *Internet and Social Media Addiction*. San Diego: ReferencePoint, 2015.

Patricia D. Netzley, *Is Online Addiction a Serious Problem?* San Diego: ReferencePoint, 2014.

Louis Peterson, *Disconnect*. Victoria, BC, Canada: Orca, 2012.

Clive Thompson, *Smarter than You Think: How Technology Is Changing Our Minds for the Better*. New York: Penguin, 2014.

Sherry Turkle, *Alone Together: Why We Expect More from Technology and Less from Each Other*. New York: Basic, 2011.

Online Articles

Jack Flanagan, "The Psychology of Video Game Addiction," *Week*, February 6, 2014. http://theweek.com/articles /451660/psychology-video-game-addiction.

Susan M. Snyder, "Colleges Begin Confronting a Surge in Potential Internet Addicts," Raw Story, February 15, 2016. www.rawstory.com/2016/02/colleges-begin-confronting-a-surge-in-potential-internet-addicts.

Jennifer Soong, "When Technology Addiction Takes Over Your Life," WebMD. www.webmd.com/mental-health/addiction/features/when-technology-addiction-takes-over-your-life.

Websites

The Center for Internet and Technology Addiction's Internet and Technology Abuse and Addiction Tests (http://virtual-addiction.com/addiction-tests). This site allows people to test themselves for various kinds of Internet and technology addiction.

Internet Addiction Support Group (http://internet-addiction.supportgroups.com). This website provides a forum for people to discuss their struggles with Internet addiction.

INDEX

Note: Boldface page numbers indicate illustrations.

Abbott, Kate, 60–62
Aboujaoude, Elias, 23
Aceret, Ryley, 5
addiction(s)
    genetics and, 24–25
    habit vs., 5–6
    to health information, 17–18
    Internet as vehicle, not target of, 15–17
    multiple, 22–23
    personality traits associated with, 19–20
addictive personality, 19–20
Ali, Raian, 64
American Psychiatric Association (APA), 8–9, 72
Andersen, Charlotte Hilton, 53
anhedonia, 26
anxiety, over separation from cell phone, 50–52
apps
    addiction-fighting, 54–56
    as designed to be addictive, 27–31
    to prevent texting while driving, 55
Ashwood Recovery center (Boise, ID), 50
attention-deficit/hyperactivity disorder (ADHD), 36–38

Bollig, Carlee, 38
boot (rehab) camps, 62
Bournemouth University, 64
boyd, danah, 16
brain
    of addicts vs. nonaddicts, 32–33
    changes in, due to Internet addiction, 33–35
    reward-based activities and rewiring of, 35–36

Camacho, Tonya, 63
Candy Crush Saga (app), 27–29, **28**, 44, 46, 47
Cash, Hilarie, 63
cat videos, 23
CellControl app, 55
Center for Internet Addiction, 9, 10, 11, 72
    on cultural influences on online addictions, 14
Center for Internet and Technology Addiction, 63, 72
Centers for Disease Control and Prevention, 38
children, 48–49
Christie, Rebecca Colleen, 52
Clayton, Russell, 52
cognitive behavioral therapy (CBT), 60
Computers in Human Behavior, 48
cyberchondria, 17–18

depression, 26

Diagnostic and Statistical Manual of Mental Disorders (DSM), 8–9

Dickey, Megan Rose, 47

digital piracy, 48

dopamine, 36

driving
  apps to prevent texting while, 55
  online distractions and reaction times, 40–41
  use of smartphones while, 38–40

Duke University, 36

Dunckley, Victoria L., 35

emotions, can determine focus of online addiction, 18

ethical design, 58–59

Facebook addicts, 32–33

Feinberg, Ashley, 47

Fergus, Thomas, 18

Frances, Allen, 8

Friston, Karl, 35

gambling, online, 15

games, online
  addiction to, 44–45
  cost of playing, 46–47
  as designed to be addictive, 27–31

Government Highway Safety Association, 42

Graham, Paul, 60

Grogan, Philippa, 5

habit
  addiction and, 5–6
  humans naturally form, 26–27

Hokemeyer, Paul, 53

HumanFIRST Laboratory (University of Minnesota), 55

Illinois Institute for Addiction Recovery, 64–65, 73

inflection point, 5–6

Internet, anxiety over not being connected to, 50–52

Jarc, Andy, 29

Journal of Addiction Medicine, 25

Journal of Internet Addiction, 23

Journal of the American Medical Association, 37

Kearney, A.T., 16

Killeen, Peter, 38

Konnikova, Maria, 15, 16, 19, 65–66

London School of Economics, 57

Madigan, Jamie, 29

magnetic resonance imaging (MRI), 32–33

massively multiplayer online role-playing game (MMORPG), 44–45

Mauer, Charles, 38

McCartney, Lauren, 42

McIntosh, Philip, 57

Milberg, Kari Jo, 38–39

Milken Institute, 32

Montag, Christian, 25–26

Murphy, Michael, 9–10, 11

Myrick, Jessica Gall, 23

National Safety Council, 38

obesity, 32
On-Line Gamers Anonymous
 (OGA), 73
online addiction(s)
 age and, 12–13
 apps designed to fight,
  54–56
 benefits of overcoming, 59
 features encouraging, 58
 fueling illegal behavior, 48
 to games designed to be
  addictive, 27–31
 gender and, 13–14
 negative consequences of, 7
 policing of, by media
  companies, 59–60
 with sexual components,
  14–15
 similarity with drug
  addictions, 6
 situational causes of, 20–22
 social component of, 11–12
 symptoms of, 9–11
 See also treatment(s)
opinion polls. See surveys

parents
 percentage of teens hiding
  online activity from, 13
 relationship with children
  threatened by online
  addictions, 48–49
 role in children's Internet
  addictions, 16–17
Pew Research Center, 13
polls. See surveys
pornography, online, 13, 14,
 15, 50
Potenza, Marc, 7, 15

relationships, parent-child, 48

reSTART Internet and
 Technology Addiction
 Recovery, 63, 73
reward-motivated behavior, 29

Safe Kids Worldwide, 42
Saldivar, Breanne, 50
Sanford, Courtney, 40
Savane, Erickka Sy, 44
Saylor, Michael, 4
Schulson, Michael, 30–31, 58,
 60
Schwartz, Tony, 10–11
shame, associated with
 addiction, 6–7, 13, 50
shopping, online, 15, 60–61
Skinner, B.F., 29–30
smartphones
 bans on, in schools, 56–57
 obsessive use of, 53
 ownership of, 4
 use while driving, 38–40
 warning labels on, 64
surveys
 on addiction-fueled digital
  piracy, 48
 on countries with largest
  percentage of continuously
  connected people, 16
 on percentage of
  smartphone owners
  keeping devices with them
  at all times, 4
 on smartphone use while
  driving, 39–40
 of teens, on hiding online
  activity from parents, 13
 on texting as major time-
  consuming activity, 12
 of young people on texting
  while driving, 43

Tech Timeout Academic
  Challenge, 5
Teen Driver Support System,
  55
Texas A&M Transportation
  Institute, 40
texting
  developing addiction to, 5–6
  as most time-consuming
    online activity, 12
  prevalence of, among teens,
    12
  while driving, 38, 40–42
  while walking, 42
thumb injuries, 37
treatment(s)
  cognitive behavioral therapy,
    60–62
  inpatient and outpatient
    centers for, 63
Turel, Ofir, 33
Turkle, Sherry, 5, 48

Valdesolo, Piercarlo, 19
Van Cleave, Ryan, 45–46
Vandehey, Jeremy, 27, 52–53
variant rewards, 30
Volkow, Nora, 36

walking, dangers of texting
  while, 42
Ward, Adrian F., 19
warning labels, 64
Weaver, Michael, 20
Weisner, Chris, 40
Woginrich, Jenna, 59, 66
World of Warcraft (video
  game), 44–45, **46**, 52
Wright, Robert, 25–27

Yager, Christine, 40–41
Yates, Ashley, 47–48
Ying, Li, 21, 22
Young, Kimberly, 21, 22
Yue, Xiao Dong, 21, 22

PICTURE CREDITS

4A 29 95